Text copyright 2023

Published by Kregel Children's, an imprint of Kregel Publications, 2450 Oak Industrial Dr. NE, Grand Rapids, MI 49505 USA. This edition copyright 2023 by Lion Hudson IP Limited.

Design by Jacqui Crawford

A catalog record of this book is available from the British Library.

Printed in China

I SPY CHRISTMAS

Written by Deborah Lock
Illustrations by Samantha Meredith

KREGEL
CHILDREN'S

Contents

A special visit

The angel Gabriel was sent by God to visit a young woman named Mary.

"Greetings!" said the angel. "God has chosen you to have a special son. You will name him Jesus."

Can you spot

1 cat

2 doves

4 bees

5 lemons

1 angel

9

Joseph's dream

Mary was to be married to Joseph.
  The angel spoke to Joseph in a dream.
  "Look after Mary and her special son,"
the angel told him.

Can you spot

1 dog

1 hammer

2 mice

1 spider

1 moon

11

To Bethlehem

Mary and Joseph lived in Nazareth.
   The Roman emperor wanted to know
how many people lived in his empire.
   Mary and Joseph had to travel
to Bethlehem to be counted.

Can you spot

1 donkey

1 boat

2 rabbits

3 palm trees

5 butterflies

No room

The town of Bethlehem was full of people.
There was no room for Mary and Joseph to stay.
Mary was going to have her baby soon.

Can you spot

1 basket of bread

1 girl holding a rug

3 rats

6 oranges

1 inn sign

Baby Jesus

Mary and Joseph found a place to stay
where the animals were kept.
Jesus was born there.
Mary laid baby Jesus
in the manger.

Can you spot

baby Jesus

3 lamps

1 purple jug

2 goats

3 chicks

17

A starry night

Some shepherds were looking after their sheep.
Suddenly, an angel stood before them.
"I bring you good news," said the angel.
"A special child is born. He is God's king."

Can you spot

1 campfire

1 lamb

1 shepherd
with a crook

1 wolf

1 owl

19

Praise to God

The night sky was filled with many, many, many angels.
"Glory to God," they praised.
The shepherds were amazed.

Can you spot

1 long trumpet

The angel holding a scroll

1 tambourine

1 harp

2 sheep

21

Hurry!

The shepherds hurried to Bethlehem to find the special child.

They saw baby Jesus in the manger. They were happy to see God's king on this very first Christmas!

Can you spot

4 mice

1 sleeping cat

3 sheep

2 rabbits

1 shepherd boy holding a lamb

23

A new star

Some wise men saw a new bright star in the night sky.
  "The star means a new king is born,"
they said. "Let us go and see him."

Can you spot

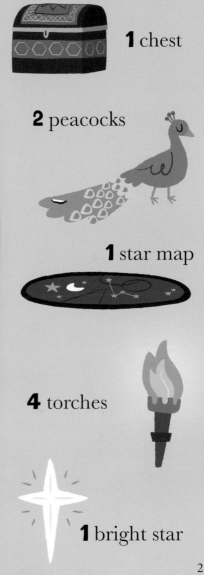

1 chest

2 peacocks

1 star map

4 torches

1 bright star

25

Follow the star!

The wise men followed the star.
The star showed them the way to Bethlehem.
The star stopped over the house where Jesus was.

Can you spot

3 camels

3 lizards

5 palm trees

1 desert fox

1 wise man's hat

Special gifts

The wise men kneeled before Jesus.
They gave him three special gifts.
The gifts were gold, frankincense, and myrrh.
Gifts for God's king!

1 toy horse

1 ball

1 bowl of fruit

2 birds

29